Wheat & Gluten Free

Recipes and Practical Advice for your Health

General Editor: Gina Steer

FLAME TREE
PUBLISHING

Publisher & Creative Director: Nick Wells
Project Editor: Sarah Goulding
Designer: Mike Spender
With thanks to: Gina Steer

This is a **FLAME TREE** Book

FLAME TREE PUBLISHING
Crabtree Hall, Crabtree Lane
Fulham, London SW6 6TY
United Kingdom
www.flametreepublishing.com

Flame Tree is part of The Foundry Creative Media Company Limited

First published 2005

Copyright © 2005 Flame Tree Publishing

05 07 09 08 06
1 3 5 7 9 10 8 6 4 2

ISBN 1 84451 117 0

A copy of the CIP data for this book is available from the British Library.

Printed in Malaysia

Contents

Living with Wheat and Gluten Intolerances   4–5

Aubergine & Yogurt Dip   6

Baby Roast Potato Salad   7

Carrot & Parsnip Terrine   8

Cheesy Vegetable & Prawn Bake   9

Chicken & Seafood Risotto   10

Chicken & White Wine Risotto   11

Chinese Fried Rice   12

Coconut Seafood   13

Creamy Chicken & Rice Pilau   14

Crown Roast of Lamb   15

Fish Roulades with Rice & Spinach   16

Fragrant Fruit Pilaf   17

Fresh Tuna Salad   18

Hot & Sour Mushroom Soup   19

Hot Salsa-filled Sole   20

Lamb & Potato Moussaka   21

Mediterranean Chowder   22

New Orleans Jambalaya   23

Potato Boulangere with Sea Bass   24

Potato, Leek & Rosemary Soup   25

Potato-stuffed Roast Poussin   26

Pumpkin & Smoked Haddock Soup   27

Seared Pancetta-wrapped Cod   28

Seared Scallop Salad   29

Seared Tuna with Pernod & Thyme   30

Shepherd's Pie   31

Slow Roast Chicken with Potatoes & Oregano   32

Smoked Haddock Rosti   33

Spanish Omelette with Smoked Cod   34

Special Rosti   35

Spiced Indian Roast Potatoes with Chicken   36

Traditional Fish Pie   37

Turkey Hash with Potato & Beetroot   38

Almond Macaroons   39

Chocolate Florentines   40

Chocolate Mousse Cake   41

Chocolate Roulade   42

Coconut Sorbet with Mango Sauce   43

Crème Brûlée with Sugared Raspberries   44

French Chocolate Pecan Torte   45

Peach & Chocolate Bake   46

Spicy White Chocolate Mousse   47

White Chocolate Terrine with Red Fruit Compote   48

Living with Wheat and Gluten Intolerances

Many medical conditions can be improved and made more tolerable and easier to live with by diet. This is especially true with wheat and gluten intolerance. By following a wheat and gluten free diet it is possible to live a normal life with very little pain or discomfort. An intolerance to gluten, also known as coeliac disease, is when the small intestines cannot digest gluten, a protein found in wheat, rye, oats, barley and their products. The gluten can damage the intestinal lining, which has a knock-on effect as it can result in the sufferer not being able to properly absorb any food they eat. Without an early diagnosis this can result, in the most drastic cases, in malnutrition, anaemia, osteoporosis and other complaints. Even in its mildest form it can cause much pain, discomfort and stomach upsets. It is not a contagious disease but can run in families.

There is a difference between coeliac disease and wheat intolerance. Wheat intolerance is an allergy just to wheat and all its products, and has a variety of symptoms. Sneezing, itching, rashes, watery eyes, runny nose, hay fever, coughing, headaches, breathing difficulties, digestive problems and swollen painful limbs can all be experienced.

Wheat intolerance can be diagnosed by a simple blood or skin test, whereas coeliac disease needs an intestinal biopsy, often under a mild sedation. Coeliac disease tends to affect young children and it is not uncommon to outgrow the problem. It is not detectable when the child is a very young baby and usually only becomes apparent after weaning, once other foods are introduced to the diet. Symptoms can include violent stomach cramps and pains as well as vomiting and diarrhoea. If your child is slow to put on weight, cries often, is anaemic and is generally miserable and unwell, it might well be worth experimenting with their diet, with the approval of your doctor. A great improvement can be seen simply by excluding wheat from the diet.

Coeliac disease is not only confined to children. According to The Coeliac Society, the majority of adult sufferers are diagnosed between the ages of 35–40, and this is on the increase. An adult's symptoms can be more serious, including weight loss, vomiting, diarrhoea or (conversely) constipation, anaemia (which leads to tiredness and lethargy), flatulence, mouth ulcers, painful joints, depression and, in some cases, infertility.

Wheat as well as oats, rye and barley need to be eliminated from the diet in order to alleviate this intolerance. This can be very hard, as a huge number of foods have 'hidden' sources of gluten. The most obvious things to avoid are bread, biscuits, cakes, pastries, many breakfast cereals, pasta, pizza, pies and some meat products (cereal-based ingredients containing wheat can be used as a bulk filler). When buying convenience foods, it is important that the ingredient list is read very carefully. Also bear in mind that when first embarking on this kind of diet, it will be necessary to check the larder and freezer so that any foods containing the offending gluten or wheat can be removed.

Although this rules out many foods, it is not all doom and gloom. There is a growing range of wheat and gluten free products available from most large supermarkets, health food shops and over the internet, including bread, pasta, biscuits, flour and cakes. These foods have had the gluten removed and substitutes are added from other sources. Substitutes such as rice, tapioca, buckwheat and cornflour can also be used instead. The recipes in this book have been specifically designed to be wheat and gluten free, but you can use many of these substitutes when adapting your own favourite recipes. Some of the most common substitutes are detailed below.

Sugar beet fibre is the dietary fibre from the sugar beet left after the sugar has been extracted. It contains a natural balance of insoluble and soluble fibre, with the soluble fibre being nutritionally beneficial.

Rice is one of the oldest grains in the world and is grown extensively. There are many varieties and it is highly suitable for those with food intolerances as it is easily digested.

Potato starch is produced by a potato that is first cleaned and then the starch and the juices are extracted separately to produce a milky liquid. This is purified and dried, forming starch granules.

Carob beans are the pods from the carob tree originating in the Mediterranean and parts of Asia. The pods contain a high degree of natural sugars and fibre, have a low sugar content and have the added advantage of a rich vitamin and mineral content.

Xanthan gum is produced by the fermentation of sugar with friendly bacteria. It is often mixed with corn syrup.

Buckwheat is no relation to wheat and is a member of the rhubarb family. The flowers are harvested after ripening and the buckwheat or seeds are removed and can be milled to provide a fine flour, or simply boiled.

Maize or corn contains no wheat or gluten and can be found in a variety of products, from oil and flour to breakfast cereals.

Tapioca comes from the cassava tree and is from the inner part of the root. Grown in Central America, Brazil and Africa it forms an integral part of the diet of these people.

Gram or channa dal comes from the chick pea family. It can be milled into a fine yellow flour, rich in natural goodness and a gluten-free source of protein and fibre.

Recent research has also shown that some sufferers can eat oats as well, but it is strongly recommended that you talk to your doctor about this first.

If following a gluten-free diet, it may be necessary to supplement it as certain vitamins and minerals may be lacking, especially the B vitamins, magnesium, phosphorous and selenium. As wheat is a complex carbohydrate it is important that sufficient fibre is eaten in order to maintain a balanced diet.

The recipes in this book have been designed to allow those intolerant of gluten and wheat to eat delicious meals that add to their quality of life. With dishes such as Seared Pancetta-wrapped Cod and Chocolate Roulade, you'll be able to experience all the joys of eating well without worrying about your health.

Some information for this introduction was taken from www.dovesfarm.co.uk

Aubergine & Yogurt Dip

Nutritional details

per 100 g

energy	36 kcals/150 kj
protein	2 g
carbohydrate	5 g
fat	1 g
fibre	0.7 g
sugar	1.4 g
sodium	trace

Ingredients
Makes 600 ml/1 pint

2 x 225 g/8 oz aubergines
1 tbsp light olive oil
1 tbsp lemon juice
2 garlic cloves, peeled and crushed
190 g jar pimentos, drained
150 ml/¼ pint low-fat
    natural yogurt
salt and freshly ground black pepper
25 g/1 oz black olives,
    pitted and chopped
225 g/8 oz cauliflower florets
225 g/8 oz broccoli florets
125 g/4 oz carrots,
    peeled and cut into
    5 cm/2 inch strips

Step-by-step guide

1 Preheat the oven to 200°C/400°F/ Gas Mark 6. Pierce the skin of the aubergines with a fork and place on a baking tray. Cook for 40 minutes or until very soft.

2 Cool the aubergines, then cut in half, and scoop out the flesh and tip into a bowl.

3 Mash the aubergine with the olive oil, lemon juice and garlic until smooth or blend for a few seconds in a food processor.

4 Chop the pimentos finely and add to the aubergine mixture.

5 When blended add the yogurt. Stir well and season to taste with salt and pepper.

6 Add the chopped olives and leave in the refrigerator to chill for at least 30 minutes.

7 Place the cauliflower and broccoli florets and carrot strips into a pan and cover with boiling water. Simmer for 2 minutes, then rinse in cold water. Drain and serve as crudités to accompany the dip.

cows' milk-free · egg-free · gluten-free · wheat-free · nut-free · vegetarian · vegan · seafood-free

Baby Roast Potato Salad

Nutritional details

per 100 g

energy	68 kcals/286 kj
protein	2 g
carbohydrate	9 g
fat	3 g
fibre	1.1 g
sugar	1.6 g
sodium	trace

Ingredients   Serves 4

350 g/12 oz small shallots
sea salt and freshly ground
    black pepper
900 g/2 lb small, even-sized
    new potatoes
2 tbsp olive oil
2 medium courgettes
2 sprigs of fresh rosemary
175 g/6 oz cherry tomatoes
150 ml/¼ pint soured cream
2 tbsp freshly snipped chives
¼ tsp paprika

Step-by-step guide

1 Preheat the oven to 200°C/400°F/ Gas Mark 6. Trim the shallots, but leave the skins on. Put in a saucepan of lightly salted boiling water along with the potatoes and cook for 5 minutes; drain.

Separate the shallots and plunge them into cold water for 1 minute.

2 Put the oil in a baking sheet lined with tinfoil or roasting tin and heat for a few minutes. Peel the skins off the shallots – they should now come away easily. Add to the baking sheet or roasting tin with the potatoes and toss in the oil to coat. Sprinkle with a little sea salt. Roast the potatoes and shallots in the preheated oven for 10 minutes.

3 Meanwhile, trim the courgettes, halve lengthways and cut into

5 cm/2 inch chunks. Add to the baking sheet or roasting tin, toss to mix and cook for 5 minutes.

4 Pierce the tomato skins with a sharp knife. Add to the sheet or tin with the rosemary and cook for a further 5 minutes, or until all the vegetables are tender. Remove the rosemary and discard. Grind a little black pepper over the vegetables.

5 Spoon into a wide serving bowl. Mix together the soured cream and chives and drizzle over the vegetables just before serving.

cows' milk-free   egg-free   gluten-free   wheat-free   nut-free   vegetarian   vegan   seafood-free

Carrot & Parsnip Terrine

Nutritional details

per 100 g

energy	49 kcals/206 kj
protein	3 g
carbohydrate	6 g
fat	2 g
fibre	2.2 g
sugar	4.2
sodium	trace

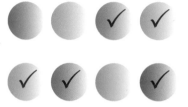

Ingredients Serves 8–10

550 g/1¼ lb carrots,
    peeled and chopped
450 g/1 lb parsnips,
    peeled and chopped
6 tbsp half-fat crème fraîche
450 g/1 lb spinach, rinsed
1 tbsp brown sugar
1 tbsp freshly chopped parsley
½ tsp freshly grated nutmeg
salt and freshly ground black pepper
6 medium eggs
sprigs of fresh basil, to garnish

For the tomato coulis:
450 g/1 lb ripe tomatoes,
    deseeded and chopped
1 medium onion,
    peeled and finely chopped

Step-by-step guide

1   Preheat the oven to 200°C/
    400°F/Gas Mark 6. Oil and line a

900 g/2 lb loaf tin with non-stick
baking paper. Cook the carrots
and parsnips in boiling salted
water for 10–15 minutes or until
very tender. Drain and purée
separately. Add 2 tablespoons of
crème fraîche to both the carrots
and the parsnips.

2   Steam the spinach for 5–10
    minutes or until very tender. Drain
    and squeeze out as much liquid
    as possible, then stir in the
    remaining crème fraîche.

3   Add the brown sugar to the carrot
    purée, the parsley to the parsnip
    mixture and the nutmeg to the
    spinach. Season all three to taste
    with salt and pepper.

4   Beat 2 eggs, add to the spinach
    and turn into the prepared tin. Add
    another 2 beaten eggs to the carrot
    mixture and layer carefully on top

of the spinach. Beat the remaining
eggs into the parsnip purée and
layer on top of the terrine.

5   Place the tin in a baking dish and
    pour in enough hot water to come
    halfway up the sides of the tin.
    Bake in the preheated oven for
    1 hour until a skewer inserted
    into the centre comes out clean.

6   Leave the terrine to cool for at
    least 30 minutes. Run a sharp
    knife around the edges. Turn out
    on to a dish and reserve.

7   Make the tomato coulis by
    simmering the tomatoes and
    onions together for 5–10 minutes
    until slightly thickened.

8   Season to taste. Blend well in a
    liquidiser or food processor and
    serve as an accompaniment to the
    terrine. Garnish with sprigs of
    basil and serve.

cows' milk-free   ✓ egg-free   ✓ gluten-free   ✓ wheat-free   ✓ nut-free   ✓ vegetarian   ✓ vegan   seafood-free

Cheesy Vegetable & Prawn Bake

Nutritional details

per 100 g

energy	94 kcals/395 kj
protein	8 g
carbohydrate	6 g
fat	4 g
fibre	1 g
sugar	1 g
sodium	0.4 g

Ingredients   Serves 4

175 g/6 oz long-grain rice
salt and freshly ground
    black pepper
1 garlic clove,
    peeled and crushed
1 large egg, beaten
3 tbsp freshly shredded basil
4 tbsp Parmesan cheese, grated
125 g/4 oz baby asparagus
    spears, trimmed
150 g/5 oz baby
    carrots, trimmed
150 g/5 oz fine green
    beans, trimmed
150 g/5 oz cherry tomatoes
175 g/6 oz peeled prawns,
    thawed if frozen
125 g/4 oz mozzarella cheese,
    thinly sliced

Step-by-step guide

1 Preheat the oven to 200°C/400°F/ Gas Mark 6, about 10 minutes before required. Cook the rice in lightly salted boiling water for 12–15 minutes or until tender, then drain. Stir in the garlic, beaten egg, shredded basil, 2 tablespoons of the Parmesan cheese and season to taste with salt and pepper. Press this mixture into a greased 23 cm/9 inch square ovenproof dish and reserve.

2 Bring a large saucepan of water to the boil, then drop in the asparagus, carrots and green beans. Return to the boil and cook for 3–4 minutes. Drain and leave to cool.

3 Quarter or halve the cherry tomatoes and mix them into the cooled vegetables. Spread the prepared vegetables over the rice and top with the prawns. Season to taste with salt and pepper.

4 Cover the prawns with the mozzarella and sprinkle over the remaining Parmesan cheese. Bake in the preheated oven for 20–25 minutes until piping hot and golden brown in places. Serve immediately.

cows' milk-free   egg-free   ✓ gluten-free   ✓ wheat-free   ✓ nut-free   vegetarian   vegan   seafood-free

Chicken & Seafood Risotto

Nutritional details

per 100 g

energy	152 kcals/638 kj
protein	17 g
carbohydrate	7 g
fat	6 g
fibre	0.3 g
sugar	0.8 g
sodium	0.5 g

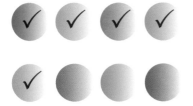

Ingredients   Serves 6–9

125 ml/4 fl oz olive oil
1.4 kg/3 lb chicken, cut into 8 pieces
350 g/12 oz spicy chorizo sausage,
  cut into 1 cm/½ inch pieces
125 g/4 oz cured ham, diced
1 onion, peeled and chopped
2 red or yellow peppers, deseeded
  and cut into 2.5 cm/1 inch pieces
4 garlic cloves, peeled and
  finely chopped
750 g/1 lb 10 oz short-grain Spanish
  rice or Arborio rice
2 bay leaves
1 tsp dried thyme
1 tsp saffron strands, lightly crushed
200 ml/7 fl oz dry white wine
1.6 litres/2¾ pints gluten-free
  chicken stock
salt and freshly ground black pepper
125 g/4 oz fresh shelled peas
450 g/1 lb uncooked prawns
36 clams and/or mussels,
  well scrubbed
2 tbsp freshly chopped parsley
fresh parsley sprigs, to garnish

Step-by-step guide

1   Heat half the oil in a 45.5 cm/
    18 inch paella pan or deep, wide
    frying pan. Add the chicken pieces
    and fry for 15 minutes, turning
    constantly, until golden. Remove
    from the pan and reserve. Add the
    chorizo and ham to the pan and
    cook for 6 minutes until crisp,
    stirring occasionally. Remove and
    add to the chicken.

2   Add the onion to the pan and
    cook for 3 minutes until beginning
    to soften. Add the peppers and
    garlic and cook for 2 minutes,
    then add to the reserved chicken,
    chorizo and ham.

3   Add the remaining oil to the pan
    and stir in the rice until well
    coated. Stir in the bay leaves,

thyme and saffron, then pour in
the wine and bubble until
evaporated, stirring and scraping
up any bits on the bottom of the
pan. Stir in the stock and bring to
the boil, stirring occasionally.

4   Return the chicken, chorizo, ham
    and vegetables to the pan, burying
    them gently in the rice. Season to
    taste with salt and pepper. Reduce
    the heat and simmer for 10
    minutes, stirring occasionally.

5   Add the peas and seafood,
    pushing them gently into the
    rice. Cover, cook over a low heat
    for 5 minutes, or until the rice and
    prawns are tender and the clams
    and mussels open – discard any
    that do not open. Stand for
    5 minutes. Sprinkle with the
    parsley and serve.

✓ cows' milk-free   ✓ egg-free   ✓ gluten-free   ✓ wheat-free   ✓ nut-free   ✓ vegetarian   ✓ vegan   ✓ seafood-free

Chicken & White Wine Risotto

Nutritional details

per 100 g

energy	195 kcals/810 kj
protein	10 g
carbohydrate	5 g
fat	12 g
fibre	trace
sugar	0.4 g
sodium	0.3 g

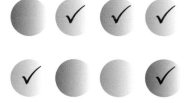

Ingredients   Serves 4–6

2 tbsp oil
125 g/4 oz unsalted butter
2 shallots, peeled and finely chopped
300 g/11 oz Arborio rice
600 ml/1 pint dry white wine
750 ml/1¼ pints gluten-free
   chicken stock, heated
350 g/12 oz skinless chicken
   breast fillets, thinly sliced
50 g/2 oz Parmesan cheese, grated
2 tbsp freshly chopped dill or parsley
salt and freshly ground black pepper

Step-by-step guide

1   Heat the oil and half the butter in a large, heavy-based saucepan over a medium-high heat. Add the shallots and cook for 2 minutes, or until softened, stirring frequently. Add the rice and cook for 2–3 minutes, stirring frequently until the rice is translucent and well coated.

2   Pour in half the wine; it will bubble and steam rapidly. Cook, stirring constantly, until the liquid is absorbed. Add a ladleful of the hot stock and cook until the liquid is absorbed. Carefully stir in the chicken.

3   Continue adding the stock, about half a ladleful at a time, allowing each addition to be absorbed before adding the next; never allow the rice to cook dry. This process

should take about 20 minutes. The risotto should have a creamy consistency and the rice should be tender, but firm to the bite.

4   Stir in the remaining wine and cook for 2–3 minutes. Remove from the heat and stir in the remaining butter with the Parmesan cheese and half the chopped herbs. Season to taste with salt and pepper. Spoon into warmed shallow bowls and sprinkle each with the remaining chopped herbs. Serve immediately.

---

cows' milk-free   ✔ egg-free   ✔ gluten-free   ✔ wheat-free   ✔ nut-free   vegetarian   vegan   ✔ seafood-free

Chinese Fried Rice

Nutritional details

per 100 g

energy	153 kcals/638 kj
protein	6 g
carbohydrate	16 g
fat	7 g
fibre	1.3 g
sugar	0.9 g
sodium	0.2 g

Ingredients   Serves 4

450 g/1 lb long-grain rice
2 tbsp groundnut oil
50 g/2 oz smoked bacon, chopped
2 garlic cloves, peeled and
    finely chopped
1 tsp freshly grated root ginger
125 g/4 oz frozen peas, thawed
2 medium eggs, beaten
125 g/4 oz beansprouts
salt and freshly ground black pepper

To garnish:
50 g/2 oz roasted
    peanuts, chopped
3 spring onions, trimmed and
    finely chopped

Step-by-step guide

1 Wash the rice in several changes
of water until it runs relatively
clear. Drain well. Put into a

saucepan or flameproof casserole
dish with a tight-fitting lid. Pour in
enough water to cover the rice by
about 1 cm/½ inch. Add salt and
bring to the boil. As soon as the
water boils, cover the saucepan,
reduce the heat as low as possible
and cook for 10 minutes. Remove
from the heat and leave to stand
for a further 10 minutes. Do not
lift the lid while cooking. Leave
until cold, then stir with a fork.

2 Heat a wok, add the oil and when
hot, add the smoked bacon. Stir-
fry for 1 minute before adding the
garlic and ginger, then stir-fry for a
further 30 seconds.

3 Add the cooked rice and peas to
the wok. Stir-fry over a high heat
for 5 minutes.

4 Add the eggs and the beansprouts
and continue to stir-fry for a
further 2 minutes until the eggs
have set. Season to taste with salt
and pepper. Spoon the mixture
onto a serving plate and garnish
with the peanuts and spring
onions. Serve hot or cold.

✓ cows' milk-free   ✓ egg-free   ✓ gluten-free   ✓ wheat-free   ✓ nut-free   ✓ vegetarian   ✓ vegan   ✓ seafood-free

Coconut Seafood

Nutritional details

per 100 g

energy	125 kcals/527 kj
protein	8 g
carbohydrate	12 g
fat	5 g
fibre	0.2 g
sugar	0.3 g
sodium	0.5 g

✓ ✓ ✓ ✓

✓ ○ ○ ○

Ingredients   Serves 4

2 tbsp sunflower oil
450 g/1 lb raw king
    prawns, peeled
2 bunches spring onions,
    trimmed and thickly sliced
1 garlic clove,
    peeled and chopped
2.5 cm/1 inch piece fresh root
    ginger, peeled and cut
    into matchsticks
125 g/4 oz fresh shiitake
    mushrooms, rinsed and halved
150 ml/¼ pint dry white wine
200 ml/7 fl oz carton
    coconut cream
4 tbsp freshly chopped coriander
salt and freshly ground
    black pepper
freshly cooked fragrant
    Thai rice

Step-by-step guide

1 Heat a large wok, add the oil and heat until it is almost smoking, swirling the oil around the wok to coat the sides. Add the prawns and stir-fry over a high heat for 4–5 minutes, or until browned on all sides. Using a slotted spoon, transfer the prawns to a plate and keep warm in a low oven.

2 Add the spring onions, garlic and ginger to the wok and stir-fry for 1 minute. Add the mushrooms and stir-fry for a further 3 minutes. Using a slotted spoon, transfer the mushroom mixture to a plate and keep warm in a low oven.

3 Add the wine and coconut cream to the wok, bring to the boil and boil rapidly for 4 minutes, until reduced slightly.

4 Return the mushroom mixture and prawns to the wok, bring back to the boil, then simmer for 1 minute, stirring occasionally, until piping hot. Stir in the freshly chopped coriander and season to taste with salt and pepper. Serve immediately with the freshly cooked fragrant Thai rice.

✓ cows' milk-free   ✓ egg-free   ✓ gluten-free   ✓ wheat-free   ✓ nut-free   ✓ vegetarian   ✓ vegan   ✓ seafood-free

Creamy Chicken & Rice Pilau

Nutritional details

per 100 g

energy	205 kcals/854 kj
protein	10 g
carbohydrate	11 g
fat	14 g
fibre	0.3 g
sugar	3.9 g
sodium	trace

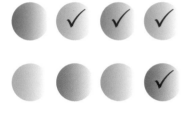

Ingredients   Serves 4–6

350 g/12 oz basmati rice
salt and freshly ground black pepper
50 g/2 oz butter
100 g/3½ oz flaked almonds
75 g/3 oz unsalted shelled
  pistachio nuts
4–6 skinless chicken breast fillets,
  each cut into 4 pieces
2 tbsp vegetable oil
2 medium onions,
  peeled and thinly sliced
2 garlic cloves, peeled and finely chopped
2.5 cm/1 inch piece of fresh root
  ginger, finely chopped
6 green cardamom pods, lightly crushed
4–6 whole cloves
2 bay leaves
1 tsp ground coriander
½ tsp cayenne pepper, or to taste
225 ml/8 fl oz natural yogurt
225 ml/8 fl oz double cream
225 g/8 oz seedless green grapes,
  halved if large
2 tbsp freshly chopped coriander or mint

Step-by-step guide

1 Bring a saucepan of lightly salted water to the boil. Gradually pour in the rice, then return to the boil and simmer for about 12 minutes until tender. Drain, rinse under cold water and reserve.

2 Heat the butter in a large, deep frying pan over a medium-high heat. Add the almonds and pistachios and cook for about 2 minutes, stirring constantly, until golden. Using a slotted spoon, transfer to a plate.

3 Add the chicken pieces to the pan and cook for 5 minutes, or until golden, turning once. Remove from the pan and reserve. Add the oil to the pan and cook the onions for 10 minutes, or until golden, stirring frequently. Stir in the garlic, ginger and spices and cook for 2–3 minutes, stirring.

4 Add 2–3 tablespoons of the yogurt and cook, stirring until the moisture evaporates. Continue adding the yogurt in this way until it is used up.

5 Return the chicken and nuts to the pan and stir. Stir in 125 ml/ 4 fl oz of boiling water and season to taste with salt and pepper. Cook, covered, over a low heat for 10 minutes until the chicken is tender. Stir in the cream, grapes and half the herbs. Gently fold in the rice. Heat through for 5 minutes and sprinkle with the remaining herbs, then serve.

cows' milk-free ✓ egg-free ✓ gluten-free ✓ wheat-free ✓ nut-free vegetarian vegan ✓ seafood-free

Crown Roast of Lamb

Nutritional details

per 100 g

energy	147 kcals/617 kj
protein	6 g
carbohydrate	17 g
fat	7 g
fibre	2 g
sugar	2.7 g
sodium	trace

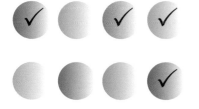

Ingredients   Serves 6

1 lamb crown roast
salt and freshly ground
    black pepper
1 tbsp sunflower oil
1 small onion, peeled and
    finely chopped
2–3 garlic cloves,
    peeled and crushed
2 celery stalks, trimmed and
    finely chopped
125 g/4 oz cooked mixed basmati
    and wild rice
75 g/3 oz ready-to-eat-dried
    apricots, chopped
50 g/2 oz pine nuts, toasted
1 tbsp finely grated orange rind
2 tbsp freshly chopped coriander
1 small egg, beaten
freshly roasted potatoes
    and green vegetables,
    to serve

Step-by-step guide

1 Preheat the oven to 180°C/350°F/ Gas Mark 4, about 10 minutes before roasting. Wipe the crown roast and season the cavity with salt and pepper. Place in a roasting tin and cover the ends of the bones with small pieces of tinfoil.

2 Heat the oil in a small saucepan and cook the onion, garlic and celery for 5 minutes, then remove the saucepan from the heat. Add the cooked rice with the apricots, pine nuts, orange rind and coriander. Season with salt and pepper, then stir in the egg and mix well.

3 Carefully spoon the prepared stuffing into the cavity of the lamb, then roast in the preheated oven for 1–1½ hours. Remove the lamb from the oven and remove and discard the tinfoil from the bones. Return to the oven and continue to cook for a further 15 minutes, or until cooked to personal preference.

4 Remove from the oven and leave to rest for 10 minutes before serving with the roast potatoes and freshly cooked vegetables.

✓ cows' milk-free   ✓ egg-free   ✓ gluten-free   ✓ wheat-free   ✓ nut-free   ✓ vegetarian   ✓ vegan   ✓ seafood-free

Fish Roulades with Rice & Spinach

Nutritional details

per 100 g

energy	44 kcals/184 kj
protein	7 g
carbohydrate	2 g
fat	1 g
fibre	1.1 g
sugar	1 g
sodium	trace

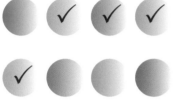

Ingredients Serves 4

4 x 175 g/6 oz lemon sole, skinned
salt and freshly ground black pepper
1 tsp fennel seeds
75 g/3 oz long-grain rice, cooked
150 g/5 oz white crab meat,
  fresh or canned
125 g/4 oz baby spinach,
  washed and trimmed
5 tbsp dry white wine
5 tbsp half-fat crème fraîche
2 tbsp freshly chopped parsley,
  plus extra to garnish
asparagus spears, to serve

Step-by-step guide

1 Wipe each fish fillet with either a clean damp cloth or kitchen paper. Place on a chopping board, skinned-side up and season lightly with salt and black pepper.

2 Place the fennel seeds in a pestle and mortar and crush lightly. Transfer to a small bowl and stir in the cooked rice. Drain the crab meat thoroughly. Add to the rice mixture and mix lightly.

3 Lay 2–3 spinach leaves over each fillet and top with a quarter of the crab meat mixture. Roll up and secure with a cocktail stick if necessary. Place into a large pan and pour over the wine. Cover and cook on a medium heat for 5–7 minutes or until cooked.

4 Remove the fish from the cooking liquid, and transfer to a serving plate and keep warm. Stir the crème fraîche into the cooking liquid and season to taste. Heat for 3 minutes, then stir in the chopped parsley.

5 Spoon the sauce on to the base of a plate. Cut each roulade into slices and arrange on top of the sauce. Serve with freshly cooked asparagus spears.

✓ cows' milk-free ✓ egg-free ✓ gluten-free ✓ wheat-free ✓ nut-free vegetarian vegan seafood-free

Fragrant Fruit Pilaf

Nutritional details

per 100 g

energy	197 kcals/825 kj
protein	10 g
carbohydrate	20 g
fat	8 g
fibre	1.2 g
sugar	7.7 g
sodium	0.2 g

Ingredients   Serves 4–6

50 g/2 oz butter
6 green cardamom pods
1 cinnamon stick
2 bay leaves
450 g/1 lb basmati rice
600 ml/1 pint gluten-free
    chicken stock
1 onion, peeled and
    finely chopped
50 g/2 oz flaked almonds
50 g/2 oz shelled pistachios,
    roughly chopped
125 g/4 oz ready-to-eat dried figs,
    roughly chopped
50 g/2 oz ready-to-eat dried
    apricots, roughly chopped
275 g/10 oz skinless chicken breast
    fillets, cut into chunks
salt and freshly ground
    black pepper
fresh parsley or coriander leaves,
    to garnish

Step-by-step guide

1   Melt half the butter in a saucepan or casserole dish with a tight-fitting lid. Add the cardamom pods and cinnamon stick and cook for about 30 seconds before adding the bay leaves and rice. Stir well to coat the rice in the butter and add the stock. Bring to the boil, cover tightly and cook very gently for 15 minutes. Remove from the heat and leave to stand for a further 5 minutes.

2   Melt the remaining butter in a wok and when foaming, add the onion, flaked almonds and pistachios. Stir-fry for 3–4 minutes until the nuts are beginning to brown. Remove and reserve.

3   Reduce the heat slightly and add the dried figs, apricots and chicken and continue stir-frying for a further 7–8 minutes until the chicken is cooked through. Add the nut mixture and toss to mix.

4   Remove from the heat, then remove the cinnamon stick and bay leaves. Add the cooked rice and stir together well to mix. Season to taste with salt and pepper. Garnish with parsley or coriander leaves and serve immediately.

cows' milk-free   ✓ egg-free   ✓ gluten-free   ✓ wheat-free   nut-free   vegetarian   vegan   ✓ seafood-free

Fresh Tuna Salad

Nutritional details

per 100 g

energy	156 kcals/646 kj
protein	13 g
carbohydrate	3 g
fat	8 g
fibre	0.1 g
sugar	0.2 g
sodium	trace

Ingredients — Serves 4

225 g/8 oz mixed salad leaves
225 g/8 oz baby cherry tomatoes, halved lengthways
125 g/4 oz rocket leaves, washed
2 tbsp olive oil
550 g/1¼ lb boned tuna steaks, each cut into 4 small pieces
50 g/2 oz piece fresh Parmesan cheese

For the dressing:
8 tbsp olive oil
grated zest and juice of 2 small lemons
1 tbsp gluten-free wholegrain mustard
salt and freshly ground black pepper

Step-by-step guide

1 Wash the salad leaves and place in a large salad bowl with the cherry tomatoes and rocket and reserve.

2 Heat the wok, then add the oil and heat until almost smoking. Add the tuna, skin-side down, and cook for 4–6 minutes, turning once during cooking, or until cooked and the flesh flakes easily. Remove from the heat and leave to stand in the juices for 2 minutes before removing.

3 Meanwhile, make the dressing. Place the olive oil, lemon zest and juices and mustard in a small bowl or screw-topped jar and whisk or shake until well blended. Season to taste with salt and pepper.

4 Transfer the tuna to a clean chopping board and flake, then add it to the salad and toss lightly.

5 Using a swivel blade vegetable peeler, peel the piece of Parmesan cheese into shavings. Divide the salad between four large serving plates, drizzle the dressing over the salad, then scatter with the Parmesan shavings.

cows' milk-free ✓ egg-free ✓ gluten-free ✓ wheat-free ✓ nut-free ✓ vegetarian vegan seafood-free

Hot & Sour Mushroom Soup

Nutritional details

per 100 g

energy	110 kcals/458 kj
protein	3 g
carbohydrate	14 g
fat	5 g
fibre	0.2 g
sugar	2.6 g
sodium	0.3 g

Ingredients   Serves 4

4 tbsp sunflower oil
3 garlic cloves, peeled and
    finely chopped
3 shallots, peeled and
    finely chopped
2 large red chillies, deseeded
    and finely chopped
1 tbsp soft brown sugar
large pinch of salt
1 litre/1¾ pints gluten-free
    vegetable stock
250 g/9 oz Thai fragrant rice
5 kaffir lime leaves, torn
grated rind and juice of 1 lemon
250 g/9 oz oyster mushrooms,
    wiped and cut into pieces
2 tbsp freshly chopped coriander

To garnish:

2 green chillies, deseeded
    and finely chopped
3 spring onions, trimmed and
    finely chopped

Step-by-step guide

1   Heat the oil in a frying pan, add the garlic and shallots and cook until golden brown and starting to crisp. Remove from the pan and reserve. Add the chillies to the pan and cook until they start to change colour.

2   Place the garlic, shallots and chillies in a food processor or blender and blend to a smooth purée with 150 ml/¼ pint water. Pour the purée back into the pan, add the sugar with a large pinch of salt, then cook gently, stirring, until dark in colour. Take care not to burn the mixture.

3   Pour the stock into a large saucepan and add the garlic purée, rice, lime leaves and the lemon rind and juice. Bring to the boil, then reduce the heat, cover and simmer gently for about 10 minutes.

4   Add the mushrooms and simmer for a further 10 minutes, or until the mushrooms and rice are tender. Remove the lime leaves, stir in the chopped coriander and ladle into bowls. Place the chopped green chillies and spring onions in small bowls and serve separately to sprinkle on top of the soup.

cows' milk-free ✓ egg-free ✓ gluten-free ✓ wheat-free ✓ nut-free ✓ vegetarian ✓ vegan ✓ seafood-free

Hot Salsa-filled Sole

Nutritional details

per 100 g

energy	73 kcals/305 kj
protein	12 g
carbohydrate	4 g
fat	1 g
fibre	trace
sugar	0.3 g
sodium	trace

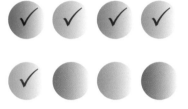

Ingredients   Serves 4

8 x 175 g/6 oz lemon
    sole fillets, skinned
150 ml/¼ pint orange juice
2 tbsp lemon juice

For the salsa:
1 small mango
8 cherry tomatoes, quartered
1 small red onion, peeled
    and finely chopped
pinch of sugar
1 red chilli
2 tbsp rice vinegar
zest and juice of 1 lime
1 tbsp olive oil
sea salt and freshly ground
    black pepper
2 tbsp freshly chopped mint
lime wedges, to garnish
salad leaves, to serve

Step-by-step guide

1 First make the salsa. Peel the mango and cut the flesh away from the stone. Chop finely and place in a small bowl. Add the cherry tomatoes to the mango together with the onion and sugar.

2 Cut the top of the chilli. Slit down the side and discard the seeds and the membrane (the skin to which the seeds are attached). Finely chop the chilli and add to the mango mixture with the vinegar, lime zest, juice and oil. Season to taste with salt and pepper. Mix thoroughly and leave to stand for 30 minutes to allow the flavours to develop.

3 Lay the fish fillets on a board, skinned-side up, and pile the salsa on the tail end of the fillets. Fold the fillets in half, season and place in a large shallow frying pan. Pour over the orange and lemon juice.

4 Bring to a gentle boil, then reduce the heat to a simmer. Cover and cook on a low heat for 7–10 minutes, adding a little water if the liquid is evaporating. Remove the cover, add the mint and cook uncovered for a further 3 minutes. Garnish with lime wedges and serve immediately with the salad.

cows' milk-free   egg-free   gluten-free   wheat-free   nut-free   vegetarian   vegan   seafood-free

Lamb & Potato Moussaka

Nutritional details

per 100 g

energy	112 kcals/466 kj
protein	6 g
carbohydrate	7 g
fat	7 g
fibre	0.3 g
sugar	0.8 g
sodium	trace

Ingredients   Serves 4

700 g/1½ lb cooked roast lamb
700 g/1½ lb potatoes, peeled
125 g/4 oz butter
1 large onion, peeled and chopped
2–4 garlic cloves,
    peeled and crushed
3 tbsp tomato purée
1 tbsp freshly chopped parsley
salt and freshly ground black pepper
3–4 tbsp olive oil
2 medium aubergines,
    trimmed and sliced
4 medium tomatoes, sliced
2 medium eggs
300 ml/½ pint gluten-free
    Greek yogurt
2–3 tbsp Parmesan cheese, grated

Step-by-step guide

1   Preheat the oven to 200°C/400°F/ Gas Mark 6, about 15 minutes before required. Trim the lamb, discarding any fat, then cut into fine cubes and reserve. Thinly slice the potatoes and rinse thoroughly in cold water, then pat dry with a clean tea towel.

2   Melt 50 g/2 oz of the butter in a frying pan and fry the potatoes, in batches, until crisp and golden. Using a slotted spoon, remove from the pan and reserve. Use a third of the potatoes to line the base of an ovenproof dish.

3   Add the onion and garlic to the butter remaining in the pan and cook for 5 minutes. Add the lamb and fry for 1 minute. Blend the tomato purée with 3 tablespoons of water and stir into the pan with the parsley and salt and pepper. Spoon over the layer of potatoes, then top with the remaining potato slices.

4   Heat the oil and the remaining butter in the pan and brown the aubergine slices for 5–6 minutes. Arrange the tomatoes on top of the potatoes, then the aubergines on top of the tomatoes. Beat the eggs with the yogurt and Parmesan cheese and pour over the aubergine and tomatoes. Bake in the preheated oven for 25 minutes, or until golden and piping hot. Serve.

Mediterranean Chowder

Nutritional details

per 100 g

energy	95 kcals/399 kj
protein	11 g
carbohydrate	7 g
fat	3 g
fibre	0.6 g
sugar	2.1 g
sodium	0.3 g

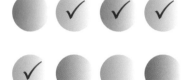

Ingredients   Serves 6

1 tbsp olive oil
1 tbsp butter
1 large onion, peeled and finely sliced
4 celery stalks, trimmed and
    thinly sliced
2 garlic cloves, peeled and crushed
1 bird's-eye chilli, deseeded and
    finely chopped
1 tbsp cornflour
225 g/8 oz potatoes,
    peeled and diced
600 ml/1 pint gluten-free fish
    or vegetable stock
700 g/1½ lb whiting or cod fillet cut
    into 2.5 cm/1 inch cubes
2 tbsp freshly chopped parsley
125 g/4 oz large peeled prawns
198 g can sweetcorn, drained
salt and freshly ground
    black pepper
150 ml/¼ pint single cream
1 tbsp freshly snipped chives

Step-by-step guide

1   Heat the oil and butter together in a large saucepan, add the onion, celery and garlic and cook gently for 2–3 minutes until softened. Add the chilli and stir in the cornflour. Cook, stirring, for a further minute.

2   Add the potatoes to the saucepan with the stock. Bring to the boil, then cover and simmer for 10 minutes. Add the fish cubes to the saucepan with the chopped parsley and cook for a further 5–10 minutes, or until the fish and potatoes are just tender.

3   Stir in the peeled prawns and sweetcorn and season to taste with salt and pepper. Pour in the cream and adjust the seasoning, if necessary.

4   Scatter the snipped chives over the top of the chowder. Ladle into six large bowls and serve immediately.

cows' milk-free   ✓ egg-free   ✓ gluten-free   ✓ wheat-free   ✓ nut-free   vegetarian   vegan   seafood-free

New Orleans Jambalaya

Nutritional details

per 100 g

energy	106 kcals/443 kj
protein	10 g
carbohydrate	6 g
fat	5 g
fibre	0.6 g
sugar	1.6 g
sodium	0.5 g

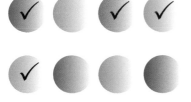

Ingredients   Serves 6–8

For the seasoning mix:
2 dried bay leaves
1 tsp salt
2 tsp cayenne pepper, or to taste
2 tsp dried oregano
1 tsp each ground white and
      black pepper, or to taste

3 tbsp vegetable oil
125 g/4 oz ham
225 g/8 oz gluten-free smoked pork
      sausage, cut into chunks
2 large onions, peeled and chopped
4 celery stalks, trimmed and chopped
2 green peppers, chopped
2 garlic cloves,
      peeled and finely chopped
350 g/12 oz fresh chicken, diced
400 g can chopped tomatoes
600 ml/1 pint gluten-free fish stock
400 g/14 oz long-grain white rice
4 spring onions, trimmed and
      coarsely chopped
275 g/10 oz raw prawns, peeled
250 g/9 oz white crab meat

Step-by-step guide

1 Mix all the seasoning ingredients in a small bowl and reserve.

2 Heat 2 tablespoons of the oil in a large flameproof casserole dish over a medium heat. Add the ham and sausage and cook, stirring often, for 7–8 minutes. Remove from the pan and reserve.

3 Add the onions, celery and peppers to the casserole and cook for about 4 minutes, or until softened, stirring occasionally. Stir in the garlic, then transfer the vegetables to a plate and reserve with the sausage.

4 Add the chicken pieces to the casserole and cook for about 4 minutes, or until beginning to colour, turning once. Stir in the seasoning mix and turn the pieces to coat well. Return the sausage and vegetables to the casserole and stir well. Add the chopped tomatoes with their juice and the stock and bring to the boil.

5 Stir in the rice and reduce the heat to low. Cover and simmer for 12 minutes. Uncover, stir in the spring onions and prawns and cook, covered, for a further 4 minutes. Add the crab and gently stir in. Cook for 2–3 minutes, or until the rice is tender. Remove from the heat, cover and leave to stand for 5 minutes before serving.

cows' milk-free   egg-free   gluten-free   wheat-free   nut-free   vegetarian   vegan   seafood-free

Potato Boulangere with Sea Bass

Nutritional details

per 100 g

energy	128 kcals/534 kj
protein	9 g
carbohydrate	9 g
fat	6 g
fibre	0.9 g
sugar	1.5 g
sodium	0.2 g

Ingredients   Serves 4

450 g/1 lb potatoes,
    peeled and thinly sliced
1 large onion, peeled and thinly sliced
salt and freshly ground black pepper
300 ml/½ pint gluten-free fish or
    vegetable stock
75 g/3 oz butter or margarine
350 g/12 oz sea bass fillets
sprigs of fresh flat leaf parsley,
    to garnish

Step-by-step guide

1 Preheat the oven to 200°C/400°F/
Gas Mark 6. Lightly grease a
shallow 1.4 litre/2½ pint baking
dish with oil or butter. Layer the
potato slices and onions alternately
in the prepared dish, seasoning
each layer with salt and pepper.

2 Pour the stock over the top,
then cut 50 g/2 oz of the butter
or margarine into small pieces
and dot over the top layer. Bake
in the preheated oven for 50–60
minutes. Do not cover the dish
at this stage.

3 Lightly rinse the sea bass fillets
and pat dry on absorbent kitchen
paper. Cook in a griddle, or heat
the remaining butter or margarine
in a frying pan and shallow fry the

fish fillets for 3–4 minutes per
side, flesh side first. Remove from
the pan with a slotted spatula and
drain on absorbent kitchen paper.

4 Remove the partly cooked potato
and onion mixture from the oven
and place the fish on the top.
Cover with tinfoil and return to the
oven for 10 minutes until heated
through. Garnish with sprigs of
parsley and serve immediately.

✓ cows' milk-free   ✓ egg-free   ✓ gluten-free   ✓ wheat-free   ✓ nut-free   ✓ vegetarian   ✓ vegan   ✓ seafood-free

Potato, Leek & Rosemary Soup

Nutritional details

per 100 g

energy	80 kcals/332 kj
protein	2 g
carbohydrate	9 g
fat	4 g
fibre	1 g
sugar	2 g
sodium	0.2 g

Ingredients   Serves 4

50 g/2 oz butter
450 g/1 lb leeks,
    trimmed and finely sliced
700 g/1½ lb potatoes,
    peeled and roughly chopped
900 ml/1½ pints gluten-free
    vegetable stock
4 sprigs of fresh rosemary
450 ml/¾ pint full cream milk
2 tbsp freshly chopped parsley
2 tbsp crème fraîche
salt and freshly ground
    black pepper

Step-by-step guide

1   Melt the butter in a large saucepan, add the leeks and cook gently for 5 minutes, stirring frequently. Remove 1 tablespoon of the cooked leeks and reserve for garnishing.

2   Add the potatoes, vegetable stock, rosemary sprigs and milk. Bring to the boil, then reduce the heat, cover and simmer gently for 20–25 minutes, or until the vegetables are tender.

3   Cool for 10 minutes. Discard the rosemary, then pour into a food processor or blender and blend well to form a smooth-textured soup.

4   Return the soup to the saucepan and stir in the chopped parsley and crème fraîche. Season to taste with salt and pepper. If the soup is too thick, stir in a little more milk or water. Reheat gently without boiling, then ladle into warm soup bowls. Garnish the soup with the reserved leeks and serve immediately.

cows' milk-free   egg-free   gluten-free   wheat-free   nut-free   vegetarian   vegan   seafood-free

Potato-stuffed Roast Poussin

Nutritional details

per 100 g

energy	209 kcals/875 kj
protein	18 g
carbohydrate	5 g
fat	12 g
fibre	0.3 g
sugar	0.2 g
sodium	0.2 g

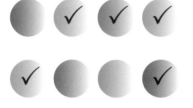

Ingredients   Serves 4

4 oven-ready poussins
salt and freshly ground black pepper
1 lemon, cut into quarters
450 g/1 lb floury potatoes, peeled and
    cut into 4 cm/1½ inch pieces
1 tbsp freshly chopped thyme
    or rosemary
3–4 tbsp olive oil
4 garlic cloves, unpeeled and
    lightly smashed
8 slices streaky bacon or Parma ham
125 ml/4 fl oz white wine
2 spring onions, trimmed
    and thinly sliced
2 tbsp double cream or crème fraîche
lemon wedges, to garnish

Step-by-step guide

1   Preheat the oven to 220°C/425°F/
    Gas Mark 7. Place a roasting tin in
    the oven to heat. Rinse the
    poussin cavities and pat dry with
    absorbent kitchen paper. Season
    the cavities with salt and pepper
    and a squeeze of lemon. Push a
    lemon quarter into each cavity.

2   Put the potatoes in a saucepan of
    lightly salted water and bring to the
    boil. Reduce the heat to low and
    simmer until just tender; do not
    overcook. Drain and cool slightly.
    Sprinkle the chopped herbs over
    the potatoes and drizzle with
    2–3 tablespoons of the oil.

3   Spoon half the seasoned potatoes
    into the poussin cavities; do not
    pack too tightly. Rub each poussin
    with a little more oil and season
    with pepper. Carefully spoon
    1 tablespoon of oil into the hot
    roasting tin and arrange the
    poussins in the tin. Spoon the
    remaining potatoes around the
    edge and sprinkle over the garlic.

4   Roast the poussins in the
    preheated oven for 30 minutes,
    or until the skin is golden and
    beginning to crisp. Carefully lay the
    bacon slices over the breast of
    each poussin and continue to roast
    for 15–20 minutes until crisp and
    the poussins are cooked through.

5   Transfer the poussins and
    potatoes to a serving platter and
    cover loosely with tinfoil. Skim off
    the fat from the juices. Place the
    tin over a medium heat and add
    the wine and spring onions. Cook
    briefly, scraping the bits from the
    bottom of the tin. Whisk in the
    cream or crème fraîche and
    bubble for 1 minute, or until
    thickened. Garnish the poussins
    with lemon wedges, and serve
    with the creamy gravy.

✓ cows' milk-free ✓ egg-free ✓ gluten-free ✓ wheat-free ✓ nut-free ✓ vegetarian ✓ vegan ✓ seafood-free

Pumpkin & Smoked Haddock Soup

Nutritional details

per 100 g

energy	58 kcals/246 kj
protein	4 g
carbohydrate	6 g
fat	1.7 g
fibre	0.9 g
sugar	1.8 g
sodium	0.3 g

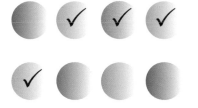

Ingredients   Serves 4–6

2 tbsp olive oil
1 medium onion,
    peeled and chopped
2 garlic cloves,
    peeled and chopped
3 celery stalks,
    trimmed and chopped
700 g/1½ lb pumpkin, peeled,
    deseeded and cut into chunks
450 g/1 lb potatoes, peeled and cut
    into chunks
750 ml/1¼ pints gluten-free
    chicken stock, heated
125 ml/4 fl oz dry sherry
200 g/7 oz smoked haddock fillet
150 ml/¼ pint milk
freshly ground black pepper
2 tbsp freshly chopped parsley

Step-by-step guide

1 Heat the oil in a large heavy-based
saucepan and gently cook the

onion, garlic, and celery for about
10 minutes. This will release the
sweetness but not colour the
vegetables. Add the pumpkin and
potatoes to the saucepan and stir
to coat the vegetables with the oil.

2 Gradually pour in the stock and
bring to the boil. Cover, then
reduce the heat and simmer for
25 minutes, stirring occasionally.
Stir in the dry sherry, then remove
the saucepan from the heat and
leave to cool for 5–10 minutes.

3 Blend the mixture in a food
processor or blender to form
a chunky purée and return to
the saucepan.

4 Meanwhile, place the fish in a
shallow frying pan. Pour in the
milk with 3 tablespoons
of water and bring to almost
boiling point. Reduce the heat,
cover, and simmer for 6 minutes,
or until the fish is cooked and
flakes easily. Remove from the
heat and, using a slotted spoon,
remove the fish from the liquid,
reserving both liquid and fish.

5 Discard the skin and any bones
from the fish and flake into
pieces. Stir the fish liquid into the
soup, together with the flaked
fish. Season with freshly ground
black pepper, stir in the parsley
and serve immediately.

cows' milk-free   egg-free   gluten-free   wheat-free   nut-free   vegetarian   vegan   seafood-free

Seared Pancetta-wrapped Cod

Nutritional details

per 100 g

energy	85 kcals/359 kj
protein	11 g
carbohydrate	5 g
fat	2 g
fibre	0.9 g
sugar	0.9 g
sodium	0.3 g

Ingredients   Serves 4

4 x 175 g/6 oz thick cod fillets
4 very thin slices of pancetta
3 tbsp capers in vinegar
1 tbsp of vegetable
   or sunflower oil
2 tbsp lemon juice
1 tbsp olive oil
freshly ground black pepper
1 tbsp freshly chopped parsley,
   to garnish

To serve:
freshly cooked vegetables
new potatoes

Step-by-step guide

1 Wipe the cod fillets and wrap each one with the pancetta. Secure each fillet with a cocktail stick and reserve.

2 Drain the capers and soak in cold water for 10 minutes to remove any excess salt, then drain and reserve.

3 Heat the oil in a large frying pan and sear the wrapped pieces of cod fillet for about 3 minutes on each side, turning carefully with a fish slice so as not to break up the fish.

4 Lower the heat then continue to cook for 2–3 minutes or until the fish is cooked thoroughly.

5 Meanwhile, place the reserved capers, lemon juice and olive oil into a small saucepan. Grind over the black pepper.

6 Place the saucepan over a low heat and bring to a gentle simmer, stirring continuously for 2–3 minutes.

7 Once the fish is cooked, garnish with the parsley and serve with the warm caper dressing, freshly cooked vegetables and new potatoes.

✓ cows' milk-free   ✓ egg-free   ✓ gluten-free   ✓ wheat-free   ✓ nut-free   ✓ vegetarian   ✓ vegan   ✓ seafood-free

Seared Scallop Salad

Nutritional details

per 100 g

energy	116 kcals/483 kj
protein	6 g
carbohydrate	8 g
fat	6 g
fibre	1.4 g
sugar	6.1 g
sodium	0.1 g

Ingredients   Serves 4

12 king (large) scallops
1 tbsp butter
2 tbsp orange juice
2 tbsp balsamic vinegar
1 tbsp clear honey
2 ripe pears, washed
125 g/4 oz rocket
125 g/4 oz watercress
50 g/2 oz walnuts
freshly ground black pepper

Step-by-step guide

1   Clean the scallops, removing the thin black vein from around the white meat and coral. Rinse thoroughly and dry on absorbent kitchen paper.

2   Cut into 2–3 thick slices, depending on the scallop size.

3   Heat a griddle pan or heavy-based frying pan, then when hot, add the butter and allow to melt.

4   Once melted, sear the scallops for 1 minute on each side or until golden. Remove from the pan and reserve.

5   Briskly whisk together the orange juice, balsamic vinegar and honey to make the dressing and reserve.

6   With a small, sharp knife carefully cut the pears into quarters, core then cut into chunks.

7   Mix the rocket leaves, watercress, pear chunks and walnuts. Pile on to serving plates and top with the scallops.

8   Drizzle over the dressing and grind over plenty of black pepper. Serve immediately.

✔ cows' milk-free   ✔ egg-free   ✔ gluten-free   ✔ wheat-free   ✔ nut-free   ✔ vegetarian   ✔ vegan   ✔ seafood-free

Seared Tuna with Pernod & Thyme

Nutritional details

per 100 g

energy	123 kcals/515 kj
protein	21 g
carbohydrate	5 g
fat	1.7 g
fibre	trace
sugar	trace
sodium	trace

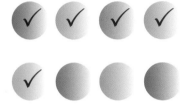

Ingredients   Serves 4

4 tuna or swordfish steaks
salt and freshly ground
    black pepper
3 tbsp Pernod
1 tbsp olive oil
zest and juice of 1 lime
2 tsp fresh thyme leaves
4 sun-dried tomatoes

To serve:
freshly cooked mixed rice
tossed green salad

Step-by-step guide

1 Wipe the fish steaks with a damp cloth or dampened kitchen paper.

2 Season both sides of the fish to taste with salt and pepper, then place in a shallow bowl and reserve.

3 Mix together the Pernod, olive oil, lime zest and juice with the fresh thyme leaves.

4 Finely chop the sun-dried tomatoes and add to the Pernod mixture.

5 Pour the Pernod mixture over the fish and chill in the refrigerator for about 2 hours, spooning the marinade occasionally over the fish.

6 Heat a griddle or heavy-based frying pan. Drain the fish, reserving the marinade. Cook the fish for 3–4 minutes on each side for a steak that is still slightly pink in the middle. Alternatively, cook the fish for 1–2 minutes longer on each side if you prefer your fish cooked through.

7 Place the remaining marinade in a small saucepan and bring to the boil. Pour the marinade over the fish and serve immediately, with the mixed rice and salad.

✓ cows' milk-free   ✓ egg-free   ✓ gluten-free   ✓ wheat-free   ✓ nut-free   ✓ vegetarian   ✓ vegan   ✓ seafood-free

Shepherd's Pie

Nutritional details

per 100 g

energy	131 kcals/548 kj
protein	9 g
carbohydrate	8 g
fat	6 g
fibre	0.8 g
sugar	1.4 g
sodium	0.1 g

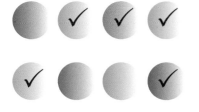

Ingredients   Serves 4

2 tbsp vegetable or olive oil
1 onion, peeled and
    finely chopped
1 carrot, peeled and
    finely chopped
1 celery stalk,
    trimmed and finely chopped
1 tbsp sprigs of fresh thyme
450 g/1 lb leftover roast lamb,
    finely chopped
150 ml/¼ pint red wine
150 ml/¼ pint gluten-free
    lamb or vegetable stock
    or leftover gravy
2 tbsp tomato purée
salt and freshly ground
    black pepper
700 g/1½ lb potatoes,
    peeled and cut into chunks
25 g/1 oz butter
6 tbsp milk
1 tbsp freshly chopped parsley
fresh herbs, to garnish

Step-by-step guide

1   Preheat the oven to 200°C/400°F/
    Gas Mark 6, about 15 minutes
    before cooking. Heat the oil in a
    large saucepan and add the onion,
    carrot and celery. Cook over a
    medium heat for 8–10 minutes until
    softened and starting to brown.

2   Add the thyme and cook briefly,
    then add the cooked lamb, wine,
    stock and tomato purée. Season
    to taste with salt and pepper and
    simmer gently for 25–30 minutes
    until reduced and thickened.
    Remove from the heat to cool
    slightly and season again.

3   Meanwhile, boil the potatoes in

plenty of salted water for 12–15
minutes until tender. Drain and
return to the saucepan over a low
heat to dry out. Remove from the
heat and add the butter, milk and
parsley. Mash until creamy, adding
a little more milk, if necessary.
Adjust the seasoning.

4   Transfer the lamb mixture
    to a shallow ovenproof dish.
    Spoon the mash over the filling
    and spread evenly to cover
    completely. Fork the surface, place
    on a baking sheet, then cook in
    the preheated oven for 25–30
    minutes until the potato topping
    is browned and the filling is
    piping hot. Garnish and serve.

Slow Roast Chicken with Potatoes & Oregano

Nutritional details

per 100 g

energy	165 kcals/689 kj
protein	6 g
carbohydrate	18 g
fat	8 g
fibre	1.3 g
sugar	0.1 g
sodium	trace

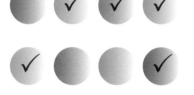

Ingredients   Serves 6

1.4–1.8 kg/3–4 lb oven-ready chicken,
   preferably free range
1 lemon, halved
1 onion, peeled and quartered
50 g/2 oz butter, softened
salt and freshly ground black pepper
1 kg/2¼ lb potatoes, peeled
   and quartered
3–4 tbsp extra virgin olive oil
1 tbsp dried oregano, crumbled
1 tsp fresh thyme leaves
2 tbsp freshly chopped thyme
fresh sage leaves, to garnish

Step-by-step guide

1 Preheat the oven to 200°C/400°F/
   Gas Mark 6. Rinse the chicken
   and dry well, inside and out, with
   absorbent kitchen paper. Rub the
   chicken all over with the lemon
   halves, then squeeze the juice
   over it and into the cavity. Put the
   squeezed halves into the cavity
   with the quartered onion.

2 Rub the softened butter all over
   the chicken and season to taste
   with salt and pepper, then put
   it in a large roasting tin, breast-
   side down.

3 Toss the potatoes in the oil,
   season with salt and pepper to
   taste and add the dried oregano
   and fresh thyme. Arrange the
   potatoes with the oil around
   the chicken and carefully pour
   150 ml/¼ pint water into one end
   of the pan (not over the oil).

4 Roast in the preheated oven for
   25 minutes. Reduce the oven
   temperature to 190°C/375°F/Gas
   Mark 5 and turn the chicken
   breast-side up. Turn the potatoes,
   sprinkle over half the fresh
   herbs and baste the chicken
   and potatoes with the juices.
   Continue roasting for 1 hour,
   or until the chicken is cooked,
   basting occasionally. If the liquid
   evaporates completely, add a little
   more water. The chicken is done
   when the juices run clear when
   the thigh is pierced with a skewer.

5 Transfer the chicken to a carving
   board and rest for 5 minutes,
   covered with tinfoil. Return the
   potatoes to the oven while the
   chicken is resting.

6 Carve the chicken into serving
   pieces and arrange on a large,
   heatproof serving dish. Arrange
   the potatoes around the chicken
   and drizzle over any remaining
   juices. Sprinkle with the remaining
   herbs and serve.

cows' milk-free   ✔ egg-free   ✔ gluten-free   ✔ wheat-free   ✔ nut-free   vegetarian   vegan   ✔ seafood-free

Smoked Haddock Rosti

Nutritional details

per 100 g

energy	77 kcals/326 kj
protein	9 g
carbohydrate	8 g
fat	1.4 g
fibre	0.7 g
sugar	1.3 g
sodium	0.4 g

Ingredients   Serves 4

450 g/1 lb potatoes,
   peeled and coarsely grated
1 large onion, peeled and
   coarsely grated
2–3 garlic cloves,
   peeled and crushed
450 g/1 lb smoked haddock
1 tbsp olive oil
salt and freshly ground black pepper
finely grated rind of ½ lemon
1 tbsp freshly chopped parsley
2 tbsp crème fraîche
mixed salad leaves, to garnish
lemon wedges, to serve

Step-by-step guide

1 Dry the grated potatoes in a clean tea towel. Rinse the grated onion thoroughly in cold water, dry in a clean tea towel and add to the potatoes.

2 Stir the garlic into the potato mixture. Skin the smoked haddock and remove as many of the tiny pin bones as possible. Cut into thin slices and reserve.

3 Heat the oil in a non-stick frying pan. Add half the potatoes and press well down in the frying pan. Season to taste with salt and pepper.

4 Add a layer of fish and a sprinkling of lemon rind, parsley and a little black pepper.

5 Top with the remaining potatoes and press down firmly. Cover with a sheet of tinfoil and cook on the lowest heat for 25–30 minutes.

6 Preheat the grill 2–3 minutes before the end of cooking time. Remove the tinfoil and place the rosti under the grill to brown. Turn out on to a warmed serving dish, and serve immediately with spoonfuls of crème fraîche, lemon wedges and mixed salad leaves.

cows' milk-free   egg-free   gluten-free   wheat-free   nut-free   vegetarian   vegan   seafood-free

Spanish Omelette with Smoked Cod

Nutritional details

per 100 g

energy	125 kcals/522 kj
protein	6 g
carbohydrate	7 g
fat	8 g
fibre	0.9 g
sugar	2.3 g
sodium	0.2 g

Ingredients   Serves 3–4

3 tbsp sunflower oil
350 g/12 oz potatoes,
    peeled and cut into 1 cm/
    ½ inch cubes
2 medium onions, peeled and
    cut into wedges
2–4 large garlic cloves,
    peeled and thinly sliced
1 large red pepper, deseeded,
    quartered and thinly sliced

125 g/4 oz smoked cod
salt and freshly ground
    black pepper
25 g/1 oz butter, melted
1 tbsp double cream

6 medium eggs, beaten
2 tbsp freshly chopped flat-leaf parsley
50 g/2 oz mature Cheddar
    cheese, grated
tossed green salad, to serve

Step-by-step guide

1   Heat the oil in a large non-stick heavy-based frying pan, add the potatoes, onions and garlic and cook gently for 10–15 minutes until golden brown, then add the red pepper and cook for 3 minutes.

2   Meanwhile, place the fish in a shallow frying pan and cover with water. Season to taste with salt and pepper and poach gently for 10 minutes. Drain and flake the fish into a bowl, add the melted butter and cream, adjust the seasoning and reserve.

3   When the vegetables are cooked, drain off any excess oil and stir in the beaten egg with the chopped parsley. Pour the fish mixture over the top and cook gently for 5 minutes, or until the eggs become firm.

4   Sprinkle the grated cheese over the top and place the pan under a preheated hot grill. Cook for 2–3 minutes until the cheese is golden and bubbling. Carefully slide the omelette onto a large plate and serve immediately with plenty of salad.

cows' milk-free   ✓ egg-free   ✓ gluten-free   ✓ wheat-free   ✓ nut-free   vegetarian   vegan   seafood-free

Special Rosti

Nutritional details

per 100 g

energy	147 kcals/611 kj
protein	5 g
carbohydrate	11 g
fat	9 g
fibre	0.9 g
sugar	1.5 g
sodium	0.2 g

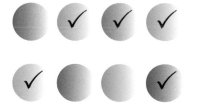

Ingredients   Serves 4

700 g/1½ lb potatoes,
    scrubbed but not peeled
salt and freshly ground
    black pepper
75 g/3 oz butter
1 large onion, peeled and
    finely chopped
1 garlic clove, peeled and crushed
2 tbsp freshly chopped parsley
1 tbsp olive oil
75 g/3 oz Parma ham,
    thinly sliced
50 g/2 oz sun-dried
    tomatoes, chopped
175 g/ 6 oz Emmenthal
    cheese, grated
mixed green salad, to serve

Step-by-step guide

1 Cook the potatoes in a large
saucepan of salted boiling water
for about 10 minutes, until just

tender. Drain in a colander, then
rinse in cold water. Drain again.
Leave until cool enough to handle,
then peel off the skins.

2 Melt the butter in a large frying
pan and gently fry the onion and
garlic for about 3 minutes until
softened and beginning to colour.
Remove from the heat.

3 Coarsely grate the potatoes into a
large bowl, then stir in the onion
and garlic mixture. Sprinkle over the
parsley and stir well to mix. Season
to taste with salt and pepper.

4 Heat the oil in the frying pan and
cover the base of the pan with half

the potato mixture. Lay the slices
of Parma ham on top. Sprinkle
with the chopped sun-dried
tomatoes, then scatter the grated
Emmenthal over the top.

5 Finally, top with the remaining
potato mixture. Cook over a low
heat, pressing down with a palette
knife from time to time, for 10–15
minutes, or until the bottom is
golden brown. Carefully invert the
rosti onto a large plate, then
carefully slide back into the pan
and cook the other side until
golden. Serve cut into wedges
with a mixed green salad.

✓ cows' milk-free ✓ egg-free ✓ gluten-free ✓ wheat-free ✓ nut-free ✓ vegetarian ✓ vegan ✓ seafood-free

Spiced Indian Roast Potatoes with Chicken

Nutritional details

per 100 g

energy	142 kcals/598 kj
protein	9 g
carbohydrate	14 g
fat	5 g
fibre	1.2 g
sugar	1.3 g
sodium	trace

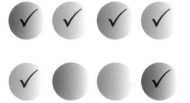

Ingredients

Serves 4

700 g/1½ lb waxy potatoes,
    peeled and cut into
    large chunks
salt and freshly ground
    black pepper
4 tbsp sunflower oil
8 chicken drumsticks
1 large Spanish onion,
    peeled and roughly chopped
3 shallots, peeled and
    roughly chopped
2 large garlic cloves,
    peeled and crushed
1 red chilli
2 tsp fresh root ginger,
    peeled and finely grated
2 tsp ground cumin
2 tsp ground coriander
pinch of cayenne pepper
4 cardamom pods, crushed
sprigs of fresh coriander,
    to garnish

Step-by-step guide

1   Preheat the oven to 190°C/375°F/
Gas Mark 5, about 10 minutes
before cooking. Parboil the potatoes
for 5 minutes in lightly salted boiling
water, then drain thoroughly and
reserve. Heat the oil in a large frying
pan, add the chicken drumsticks
and cook until sealed on all sides.
Remove and reserve.

2   Add the onions and shallots to the
pan and fry for 4–5 minutes, or
until softened. Stir in the garlic,
chilli and ginger and cook for
1 minute, stirring constantly. Stir
in the ground cumin, coriander,
cayenne pepper and crushed
cardamom pods and continue
to cook, stirring, for a
further minute.

3   Add the potatoes to the pan, then
add the chicken. Season to taste
with salt and pepper. Stir gently
until the potatoes and chicken
pieces are coated in the onion and
spice mixture.

4   Spoon into a large roasting tin
and roast in the preheated oven
for 35 minutes, or until the
chicken and potatoes are cooked
thoroughly. Garnish with fresh
coriander and serve immediately.

✓ cows' milk-free   ✓ egg-free   ✓ gluten-free   ✓ wheat-free   ✓ nut-free   ✓ vegetarian   ✓ vegan   ✓ seafood-free

Traditional Fish Pie

Nutritional details

per 100 g

energy	102 kcals/429 kj
protein	8 g
carbohydrate	10 g
fat	3 g
fibre	0.6 g
sugar	2.2 g
sodium	0.2 g

Ingredients   Serves 4

450 g/1 lb cod or coley
    fillets, skinned
450 ml/¾ pint milk
1 small onion, peeled and quartered
salt and freshly ground black pepper
900 g/2 lb potatoes,
    peeled and cut into chunks
100 g/3½ oz butter
125 g/4 oz large prawns
2 large eggs, hard-boiled
    and quartered
198 g can sweetcorn, drained
2 tbsp freshly chopped parsley
2 tbsp cornflour
50 g/2 oz Cheddar cheese, grated

Step-by-step guide

1   Preheat the oven to 200°C/400°F/ Gas Mark 6, about 15 minutes before cooking. Place the fish in a shallow frying pan, pour over 300 ml/½ pint of the milk and add the onion. Season to taste with salt and pepper. Bring to the boil and simmer for 8–10 minutes until the fish is cooked. Remove the fish with a slotted spoon and place in a 1.4 litre/ 2½ pint baking dish. Strain the cooking liquid and reserve.

2   Boil the potatoes until soft, then mash with 40 g/1½ oz of the butter and 2–3 tablespoons of the remaining milk. Reserve.

3   Arrange the prawns and sliced eggs on top of the fish, then scatter over the sweetcorn and sprinkle with the parsley.

4   Melt the remaining butter in a saucepan, then mix the cornflour with a little water and add, stirring. Whisk in the reserved cooking liquid and remaining milk. Cook for 2 minutes, or until thickened, then pour over the fish mixture and cool slightly.

5   Spread the mashed potato over the top of the pie and sprinkle over the grated cheese. Bake in the preheated over for 30 minutes until golden. Serve immediately.

cows' milk-free   ✓ egg-free   ✓ gluten-free   ✓ wheat-free   ✓ nut-free   ✓ vegetarian   ✓ vegan   seafood-free

Turkey Hash with Potato & Beetroot

Nutritional details

per 100 g

energy	135 kcals/565 kj
protein	12 g
carbohydrate	8 g
fat	6 g
fibre	0.9 g
sugar	2.3 g
sodium	0.2 g

Ingredients   Serves 4–6

2 tbsp vegetable oil
50 g/2 oz butter
4 slices streaky bacon,
    diced or sliced
1 medium onion,
    peeled and finely chopped
450 g/1 lb cooked
    turkey, diced
450 g/1 lb finely chopped
    cooked potatoes
2–3 tbsp freshly chopped parsley
2 tbsp cornflour
250 g/9 oz cooked medium
    beetroot, diced
green salad, to serve

Step-by-step guide

1   In a large, heavy-based frying pan, heat the oil and half the butter over a medium heat until sizzling. Add the bacon and cook for 4 minutes, or until crisp and golden, stirring occasionally. Using a slotted spoon, transfer to a large bowl. Add the onion to the pan and cook for 3–4 minutes, or until soft and golden, stirring frequently.

2   Meanwhile, add the turkey, potatoes, parsley and cornflour (mixed first with a little water) to the cooked bacon in the bowl. Stir and toss gently, then fold in the diced beetroot.

3   Add half the remaining butter to the frying pan and then the turkey vegetable mixture. Stir, then spread the mixture to cover the bottom of the frying pan. Cook for 15 minutes, until the underside is crisp and brown, pressing firmly with a spatula. Remove from the heat.

4   Invert a large plate over the frying pan and, holding the plate and frying pan together with an oven glove, turn the hash out onto the plate. Heat the remaining butter in the pan, slide the hash back into the pan and cook for 4 minutes, or until crisp and brown on the other side. Invert onto the plate again and serve immediately with a green salad.

✓ cows' milk-free   ✓ egg-free   ✓ gluten-free   ✓ wheat-free   ✓ nut-free   ✓ vegetarian   ✓ vegan   ✓ seafood-free

Almond Macaroons

Nutritional details

per 100 g

energy	383 kcals/1621 kj
protein	5 g
carbohydrate	72 g
fat	10 g
fibre	trace
sugar	58 g
sodium	trace

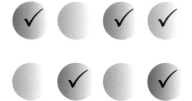

Ingredients   Makes 12

rice paper
125 g/4 oz caster sugar
50 g/2 oz ground almonds
1 tsp ground rice
2–3 drops almond essence
1 medium egg white
8 blanched almonds, halved

Step-by-step guide

1 Preheat the oven to 150°C/300°F/ Gas Mark 2, 10 minutes before baking. Line a baking sheet with the rice paper.

2 Mix the caster sugar, ground almonds, ground rice and almond essence together and reserve.

3 Whisk the egg white until stiff then gently fold in the caster sugar mixture with a metal spoon or rubber spatula.

4 Mix to form a stiff but not sticky paste. If the mixture is very sticky, add a little extra ground almonds.

5 Place small spoonfuls of the mixture, about the size of an apricot, well apart on the rice paper.

6 Place a half-blanched almond in the centre of each. Place in the preheated oven and bake for 25 minutes, or until just pale golden.

7 Remove the biscuits from the oven and leave to cool for a few minutes on the baking sheet. Cut or tear the rice paper around the macaroons to release them. Once cold, serve or otherwise store them in an airtight tin.

✓ cows' milk-free ✓ egg-free ✓ gluten-free ✓ wheat-free ✓ nut-free ✓ vegetarian ✓ vegan ✓ seafood-free

Chocolate Florentines

Nutritional details

per 100 g

energy	502 kcals/2098 kj
protein	5 g
carbohydrate	50 g
fat	34 g
fibre	0.6 g
sugar	47 g
sodium	0.1 g

Ingredients   Makes 20

125 g/4 oz butter or margarine
125 g/4 oz soft light brown sugar
1 tbsp double cream
50 g/2 oz blanched almonds,
    roughly chopped
50 g/2 oz hazelnuts,
    roughly chopped
75 g/3 oz sultanas
50 g/2 oz glacé cherries,
    roughly chopped
50 g/2 oz plain, dark chocolate,
    roughly chopped or broken
50 g/2 oz milk chocolate, roughly
    chopped or broken
50 g/2 oz white chocolate, roughly
    chopped or broken

Step-by-step guide

1 Preheat the oven to 180°C/350°F/
    Gas Mark 4, 10 minutes before
    baking. Lightly oil a baking sheet.

2 Melt the butter or margarine with
    the sugar and double cream in a
    small saucepan over a very low
    heat. Do not boil.

3 Remove from the heat and stir in
    the almonds, hazelnuts, sultanas
    and cherries.

4 Drop teaspoonfuls of the mixture
    on to the baking sheet. Transfer to
    the preheated oven and bake for
    10 minutes, until golden.

5 Leave the biscuits to cool on the
    baking sheet for about 5 minutes,
    then carefully transfer to a wire
    rack to cool.

6 Melt the plain, milk and white
    chocolates in separate bowls, either
    in the microwave following the
    manufacturers' instructions or in a
    small bowl, placed over a saucepan
    of gently simmering water.

7 Spread one third of the biscuits
    with the plain chocolate, one third
    with the milk chocolate and one
    third with the white chocolate.

8 Mark out wavy lines on the
    chocolate when almost set with
    the tines of a fork. Alternatively,
    dip some of the biscuits in
    chocolate to half coat and serve.

cows' milk-free   egg-free   gluten-free   wheat-free   nut-free   vegetarian   vegan   seafood-free

Chocolate Mousse Cake

Nutritional details

per 100 g

energy	407 kcals/1699 kj
protein	6 g
carbohydrate	36 g
fat	26 g
fibre	1 g
sugar	35 g
sodium	trace

Ingredients
Cuts into 8–10 servings

For the cake:
450 g/1 lb plain dark
    chocolate, chopped
125 g/4 oz butter, softened
3 tbsp brandy
9 large eggs, separated
150 g/5 oz caster sugar

For the chocolate glaze:
225 ml/8 fl oz double cream
225 g/8 oz plain dark
    chocolate, chopped
2 tbsp brandy
1 tbsp single cream and white
    chocolate curls, to decorate

Step-by-step guide

1 Preheat the oven to 180°C/350°F/
Gas Mark 4, 10 minutes before
baking. Lightly oil and line the bases
of two 20.5 cm/8 inch springform
tins with baking paper. Melt the
chocolate and butter in a bowl set
over a saucepan of simmering
water. Stir until smooth. Remove
from the heat and stir in the brandy.

2 Whisk the egg yolks and the sugar,
reserving 2 tablespoons of the
sugar, until thick and creamy. Slowly
beat in the chocolate mixture until
smooth and well blended. Whisk
the egg whites until soft peaks
form, then sprinkle over the
remaining sugar and continue
whisking until stiff but not dry.

3 Fold a large spoonful of the egg
whites into the chocolate mixture.
Gently fold in the remaining egg
whites. Divide about two thirds of
the mixture evenly between the tins,
tapping to distribute the mixture
evenly. Reserve the remaining one
third of the chocolate mousse
mixture for the filling. Bake in
the preheated oven for about

20 minutes, or until the cakes are
well risen and set. Remove and
cool for at least 1 hour.

4 Loosen the edges of the cake layers
with a knife. Using your fingertips,
lightly press the crusty edges
down. Pour the rest of the mousse
over one layer, spreading until
even. Carefully unclip the side,
remove the other cake from the tin
and gently invert on to the mousse,
bottom side up to make a flat top
layer. Discard the lining paper and
chill for 4–6 hours, or until set.

5 To make the glaze, melt the cream
and chocolate with the brandy in a
heavy-based saucepan and stir
until smooth. Cool until thickened.
Unclip the side of the mousse cake
and place on a wire rack. Pour over
half the glaze and spread to cover.
Allow to set, then decorate with
chocolate curls. To serve, heat the
remaining glaze and pour round
each slice, and dot with cream.

cows' milk-free ✓ egg-free ✓ gluten-free ✓ wheat-free ✓ nut-free ✓ vegetarian ✓ vegan seafood-free

Chocolate Roulade

Nutritional details

per 100 g

energy	199 kcals/842 kj
protein	3 g
carbohydrate	28 g
fat	10 g
fibre	0.6 g
sugar	25 g
sodium	trace

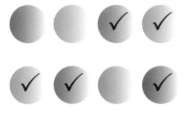

Ingredients   Serves 8

150 g/5 oz golden caster sugar
5 medium eggs, separated
50 g/2 oz cocoa powder

For the filling:

300 ml/½ pint double cream
3 tbsp whisky
50 g/2 oz creamed coconut, chilled
2 tbsp icing sugar
coarsely shredded coconut, toasted

Step-by-step guide

1 Preheat the oven to 180°C/350°F/ Gas Mark 4, 10 minutes before baking. Oil and line a 33 x 23 cm/ 13 x 9 inch Swiss roll tin with a single sheet of non-stick baking parchment. Dust a large sheet of baking parchment with 2 tablespoons of the caster sugar.

2 Place the egg yolks in a bowl with the remaining sugar, set over a saucepan of gently simmering water and whisk until pale and thick. Sift the cocoa powder into the mixture and carefully fold in.

3 Whisk the egg whites in a clean, grease-free bowl until soft peaks form. Gently add 1 tablespoon of the whisked egg whites into the chocolate mixture then fold in the remaining whites. Spoon the mixture into the prepared tin, smoothing the mixture into the corners. Bake in the preheated oven for 20–25 minutes, or until risen and springy to the touch.

4 Turn the cooked roulade out onto the sugar-dusted baking parchment and carefully peel off the lining paper. Cover with a clean, damp tea towel and leave to cool.

5 To make the filling, pour the cream and whisky into a bowl and whisk until the cream holds its shape. Grate in the chilled creamed coconut, add the icing sugar and gently stir in. Uncover the roulade and spoon about three quarters of coconut cream on the roulade and roll up. Spoon the remaining cream on the top and sprinkle with the coconut, then serve.

   ⊘ cows' milk-free ✓ egg-free ⊘ gluten-free ✓ wheat-free ✓ nut-free ✓ vegetarian ✓ vegan ⊘ seafood-free

Coconut Sorbet with Mango Sauce

Nutritional details

per 100 g

energy	188 kcals/792 kj
protein	1 g
carbohydrate	25 g
fat	11 g
fibre	trace
sugar	17 g
sodium	trace

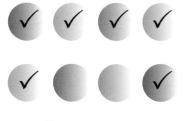

Ingredients Serves 4

2 sheets gelatine
250 g/9 oz caster sugar
600 ml/1 pint coconut milk
2 mangos, peeled, pitted and sliced
2 tbsp icing sugar
zest and juice of 1 lime

Step-by-step guide

1 Set the freezer to rapid freeze 2 hours before freezing the sorbet. Place the sheets of gelatine in a shallow dish, pour over cold water to cover and leave for 15 minutes. Squeeze out any excess moisture before use.

2 Meanwhile, place the caster sugar and 300 ml/½ pint of the coconut milk in a heavy-based saucepan and heat gently, stirring occasionally, until the sugar has dissolved. Remove from the heat.

3 Add the soaked gelatine to the saucepan and stir gently until dissolved. Stir in the remaining coconut milk. Leave until cold.

4 Pour the gelatine and coconut mixture into a freezable container and place in the freezer. Leave for at least 1 hour, or until the mixture has started to form ice crystals. Remove and beat with a spoon, then return to the freezer and continue to freeze until the mixture is frozen, beating at least twice more during this time.

5 Meanwhile, make the sauce. Place the sliced mango, icing sugar and the lime zest and juice in a food processor and blend until smooth. Spoon into a small jug.

6 Leave the sorbet to soften in the refrigerator for at least 30 minutes before serving. Serve scoops of sorbet on individual plates with a little of the mango sauce poured over. Remember to turn the freezer to its normal setting.

cows' milk-free egg-free gluten-free wheat-free nut-free vegetarian vegan seafood-free

Crème Brûlée with Sugared Raspberries

Nutritional details

per 100 g

energy	314 kcals/1302 kj
protein	3 g
carbohydrate	14 g
fat	28 g
fibre	0.5 g
sugar	13 g
sodium	trace

Ingredients   Serves 6

600 ml/1 pint fresh
    whipping cream
4 medium egg yolks
75 g/3 oz caster sugar
½ tsp vanilla essence
25 g/1 oz demerara sugar
175 g/6 oz fresh raspberries

Step-by-step guide

1 Preheat the oven to 150°C/300°F/ Gas Mark 2. Pour the cream into a bowl and place over a saucepan of gently simmering water. Heat gently but do not allow to boil.

2 Meanwhile, whisk together the egg yolks, 50 g/2 oz of the caster sugar and the vanilla essence. When the cream is warm, pour it over the egg mixture, briskly whisking until it is mixed completely.

3 Pour into six individual ramekin dishes and place in a roasting tin.

4 Fill the tin with sufficient water to come halfway up the sides of the dishes.

5 Bake in the preheated oven for about 1 hour, or until the puddings are set. To test if set, carefully insert a round bladed knife into the centre – if the knife comes out clean they are set.

6 Remove the puddings from the roasting tin and allow to cool. Chill in the refrigerator, preferably overnight.

7 Sprinkle the sugar over the top of each dish and place the puddings under a preheated hot grill.

8 When the sugar has caramelised and turned deep brown, remove from the heat and cool. Chill the puddings in the refrigerator for 2–3 hours before serving.

9 Toss the raspberries in the remaining caster sugar and sprinkle over the top of each dish. Serve with a little extra cream if liked.

cows' milk-free   ✓ egg-free   ✓ gluten-free   ✓ wheat-free   ✓ nut-free   ✓ vegetarian   ✓ vegan   seafood-free

French Chocolate Pecan Torte

Nutritional details

per 100 g

energy	490 kcals/2042 kj
protein	5 g
carbohydrate	35 g
fat	37 g
fibre	0.8 g
sugar	33 g
sodium	0.1 g

Ingredients
Cut into 16 slices

200 g/7 oz plain dark
    chocolate, chopped
150 g/5 oz butter, diced
4 large eggs
100 g/3½ oz caster sugar
2 tsp vanilla essence
125 g/4 oz pecans,
    finely ground
2 tsp ground cinnamon
24 pecan halves,
    lightly toasted,
    to decorate

For the chocolate glaze:

125 g/4 oz plain dark
    chocolate, chopped
60 g/2½ oz butter, diced
2 tbsp clear honey
¼ tsp ground cinnamon

Step-by-step guide

1 Preheat the oven to 180°C/350°F/ Gas Mark 4, 10 minutes before baking. Lightly butter and line a 20.5 x 5 cm/8 x 2 inch springform tin with non-stick baking paper. Wrap the tin in a large sheet of tinfoil to prevent water seeping in.

2 Melt the chocolate and butter in a saucepan over a low heat and stir until smooth. Remove from the heat and cool.

3 Using an electric whisk, beat the eggs, sugar and vanilla essence until light and foamy. Gradually beat in the melted chocolate, ground nuts and cinnamon, then pour into the prepared tin.

4 Set the foil-wrapped tin in a large roasting tin and pour in enough boiling water to come 2 cm/¾ inch up the sides of the tin. Bake in the preheated oven until the edge is set, but the centre is still soft when the tin is gently shaken. Remove from the oven and place on a wire rack to cool.

5 For the glaze, melt all the ingredients over a low heat until melted and smooth, then remove from the heat. Dip each pecan halfway into the glaze and set on a sheet of non-stick baking paper until set. Allow the remaining glaze to thicken slightly.

6 Remove the cake from the tin and invert. Pour the glaze over the cake, smoothing the top and spreading the glaze around the sides. Arrange the glazed pecans around the edge of the torte. Allow to set and serve.

Peach & Chocolate Bake

Nutritional details

per 100 g

energy	276 kcals/1152 kj
protein	3 g
carbohydrate	29 g
fat	17 g
fibre	0.8 g
sugar	28 g
sodium	trace

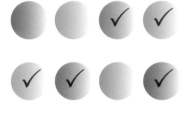

Ingredients   Serves 4

200 g/7 oz plain dark chocolate
125 g/4 oz unsalted butter
4 medium eggs, separated
125 g/4 oz caster sugar
425 g can peach slices, drained
½ tsp ground cinnamon
1 tbsp icing sugar, sifted,
    to decorate
crème fraîche, to serve

Step-by-step guide

1   Preheat the oven to 170°C/325°F/
Gas Mark 3, 10 minutes before
baking. Lightly oil a 1.7 litre/3 pint
ovenproof dish.

2   Break the chocolate and butter
into small pieces and place in a
small heatproof bowl set over a
saucepan of gently simmering
water. Ensure the water is not
touching the base of the bowl
and leave to melt. Remove the
bowl from the heat and stir
until smooth.

3   Whisk the egg yolks with the
sugar until very thick and creamy,
then stir the melted chocolate and
butter into the whisked egg yolk
mixture and mix together lightly.

4   Place the egg whites in a clean,
grease-free bowl and whisk until
stiff, then fold 2 tablespoons of
the whisked egg whites into the
chocolate mixture. Mix well, then
add the remaining egg white and
fold in very lightly.

5   Fold the peach slices and the
cinnamon into the mixture, then
spoon the mixture into the
prepared dish. Do not level the
mixture, leave a little uneven.

6   Bake in the preheated oven for
35–40 minutes, or until well risen
and just firm to the touch.
Sprinkle the bake with the icing
sugar and serve immediately with
spoonfuls of crème fraîche.

cows' milk-free   ✓ egg-free   ✓ gluten-free   ✓ wheat-free   ✓ nut-free   ✓ vegetarian   ✓ vegan   seafood-free

Spicy White Chocolate Mousse

Nutritional details

per 100 g

energy	360 kcals/1491 kj
protein	5 g
carbohydrate	18 g
fat	30 g
fibre	trace
sugar	17 g
sodium	trace

Ingredients   Serves 4–6

6 cardamom pods
125 ml/4 fl oz milk
3 bay leaves
200 g/7 oz white chocolate
300 ml/½ pint double cream
3 medium egg whites
1–2 tsp cocoa powder, sifted,
    for dusting

Step-by-step guide

1   Tap the cardamom pods lightly so they split. Remove the seeds then, using a pestle and mortar, crush lightly. Pour the milk into a small saucepan and add the crushed seeds and the bay leaves. Bring to the boil gently over a medium heat. Remove from the heat, cover and leave in a warm place for at least 30 minutes to infuse.

2   Break the chocolate into small pieces and place in a heatproof bowl set over a saucepan of gently simmering water. Ensure the water is not touching the base of the bowl. When the chocolate has melted remove the bowl from the heat and stir until smooth.

3   Whip the cream until it has slightly thickened and holds its shape, but does not form peaks. Reserve. Whisk the egg whites in a clean, grease-free bowl until stiff and standing in soft peaks.

4   Strain the milk through a sieve into the cooled, melted chocolate and beat until smooth. Spoon the chocolate mixture into the egg whites, then using a large metal spoon, fold gently. Add the whipped cream and fold in gently.

5   Spoon into a large serving dish or individual small cups. Chill in the refrigerator for 3–4 hours. Just before serving, dust with a little sifted cocoa powder and then serve.

White Chocolate Terrine with Red Fruit Compote

Nutritional details

per 100 g

energy	345 kcals/1432 kj
protein	3 g
carbohydrate	24 g
fat	27 g
fibre	0.3 g
sugar	22 g
sodium	trace

Ingredients   Serves 8

225 g/8 oz white chocolate
300 ml/½ pint double cream
225 g/8 oz full fat soft cream cheese
2 tbsp finely grated orange rind
125 g/4 oz caster sugar
350 g/12 oz mixed summer
        fruits, such as strawberries,
        blueberries and raspberries
1 tbsp Cointreau
sprigs of fresh mint, to decorate

Step-by-step guide

1   Set the freezer to rapid freeze at least 2 hours before required. Lightly oil and line a 450 g/1 lb loaf tin with clingfilm, taking care to keep the clingfilm as wrinkle free as possible. Break the white chocolate into small pieces and place in a heatproof bowl set over a saucepan of gently simmering water. Leave for 20 minutes or until melted, then remove from the heat and stir until smooth. Leave to cool.

2   Whip the cream until soft peaks form. Beat the cream cheese until soft and creamy, then beat in the grated orange rind and 50 g/2 oz of the caster sugar. Mix well, then fold in the whipped cream and then the cooled, melted white chocolate.

3   Spoon the mixture into the prepared loaf tin and level the surface. Place in the freezer and freeze for at least 4 hours or until frozen. Once frozen, remember to return the freezer to its normal setting.

4   Place the fruits with the remaining sugar in a heavy-based saucepan and heat gently, stirring occasionally, until the sugar has dissolved and the juices from the fruits are just beginning to run. Add the Cointreau.

5   Dip the loaf tin into hot water for 30 seconds and invert onto a serving plate. Carefully remove the tin and clingfilm. Decorate with sprigs of mint and serve sliced with the red fruit compote.

⊘ cows' milk-free   ✓ egg-free   ⊘ gluten-free   ✓ wheat-free   ✓ nut-free   ✓ vegetarian   ✓ vegan   ⊘ seafood-free